School - xue xiao	2
Törn - lü xing	5
Transport - jiao tong yun shu	8
Stadt - cheng shi	10
Landschop - di xing	14
Spieslokal - can guan	17
Supermarkt - chao shi	20
Drünk - yin liao	22
Eten - shi wu	23
Buernhoff - nong chang	27
Huus - fang zi	31
Wahnstuuv - ke ting	33
Köök - chu fang	35
Baadstuuv - yu shi	38
Kinnerstuuv - er tong fang	42
Tüüch - yi fu	44
Büro - ban gong shi	49
Weertschop - jing ji	51
Profeschonen - zhi ye	53
Warktüüch - gong ju	56
Musikinstrumenten - yue qi	57
Deertenpark - dong wu yuan	59
Sport - ti yu	62
Aktivitäten - huo dong	63
Familje - jia	67
Lief - shen ti	68
Krankenhuus - yi yuan	72
Nootfall - jin ji qing kuang	76
Eerd - di qiu	77
Klock - zhong biao	79
Week - zhou	80
Johr - nian	81
Formen - xing zhuang	83
Farven - yan se	84
Gegendelen - fan yi ci	85
Tallen - shu zi	88
Spraken - yu yan	90
wokeen / wat / wo - shei / shen me / zen yang	91
wo - fang wei	92

Impressum
Verlag: BABADADA GmbH, Nedderfeld 112 , 22529 Hamburg
Geschäftsführer / Verlagsleitung: Harald Hof
Druck: Books on Demand GmbH, In de Tarpen 42, 22848 Norderstedt

Imprint
Publisher: BABADADA GmbH, Nedderfeld 112 , 22529 Hamburg, Germany
Managing Director / Publishing direction: Harald Hof
Print: Books on Demand GmbH, In de Tarpen 42, 22848 Norderstedt, Germany

School

xue xiao

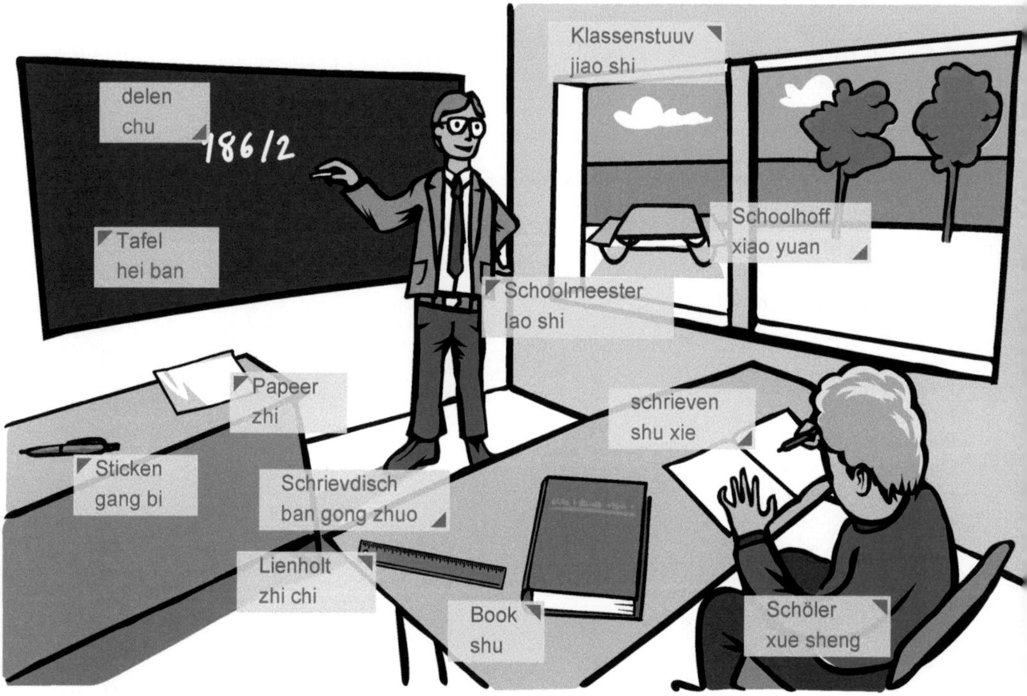

Klassenstuuv
jiao shi
delen
chu
186/2
Tafel
hei ban
Schoolhoff
xiao yuan
Schoolmeester
lao shi
Papeer
zhi
schrieven
shu xie
Sticken
gang bi
Schrievdisch
ban gong zhuo
Lienholt
zhi chi
Book
shu
Schöler
xue sheng

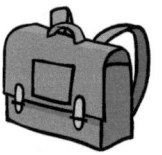

Ranzel

shu bao

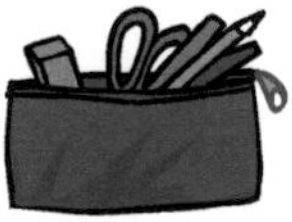

Feddermapp

qian bi he

Bleesticken

qian bi

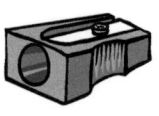

Scharpmaker

juan bi dao

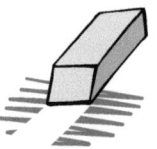

Radeergummi

xiang pi ca

Tekenblock

hua ban

Teken

tu hua

Pinsel

hua bi

Malkassen

yan liao he

Scheer

jian dao

Klever

jiao shui

Heft to'n Öven

lian xi ce

Huusopgaav

jia ting zuo ye

12

Tall

shu zi

2+2

tohooptellen

jia

5-2

aftrecken

jian

2×2

malnehmen

cheng

reken

ji suan

A

Bookstaav

zi mu

ABCDEFG HIJKLMN OPQRSTU VWXYZ

ABC

zi mu biao

hello

Woort

zi

Text
ke wen

lesen
du

Kried
fen bi

Stunn
shang ke

Klassenbook
deng ji

Pröven
kao shi

Tüügnis
zheng shu

Schooluniform
xiao fu

Utbillen
jiao yu

Nakieksel
bai ke quan shu

Universität
da xue

Mikroskop
xian wei jing

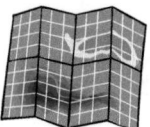

Koort
di tu

Papeerkorf
fei zhi kuang

Törn
lü xing

Hotel
jiu dian
Grand
Harbarg
qing nian lü xing she
Wesselstuuv
wai bi dui huan chu
CHANGE
Kuffer
shou ti xiang
Auto
qi che

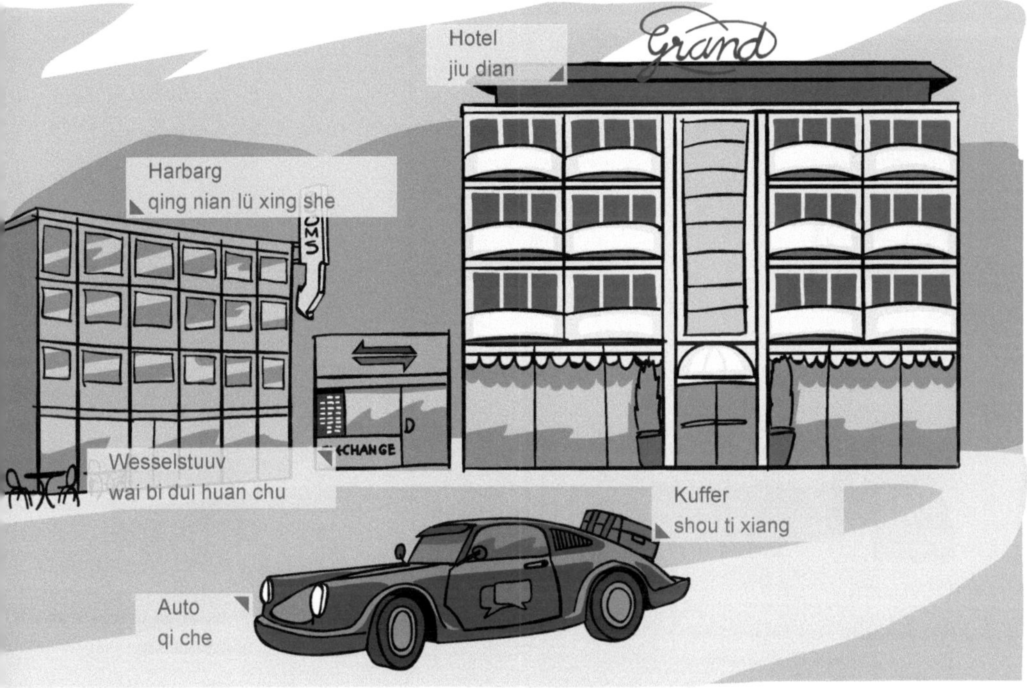

Spraak
yu yan

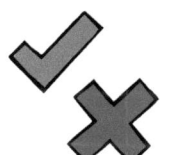

jo / ne
shi/fou

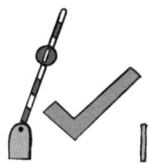

Jo
hao de

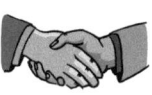

Moin
nin hao

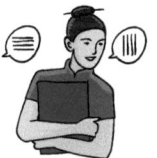

Översetter
fan yi yuan

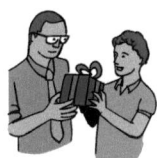

Dank ok
xie xie

Wat kost...?

......duo shao qian?

Ik verstah nich

wo bu ming bai

Problem

wen ti

Goden Avend

wan shang hao!

Moin!

zao shang hao!

Gode Nacht!

wan an!

Tschüüs

zai jian

Richt

fang xiang

Bagaasch

xing li

Tasch

bao

Rüchsack

shuang jian bao

Gast

ke ren

Stuuv

fang jian

Slaapsack

shui dai

Telt

zhang peng

Touristeninformatschoon
lü you xin xi

Strand
hai tan

Kreditkoort
xin yong ka

Fröhstück
zao can

Meddageten
wu can

Avendeten
wan can

Fohrkort
piao

Fohrstohl
dian ti

Breefmark
you piao

Grenz
bian jie

Toll
hai guan

Bottschop
da shi guan

Visum
qian zheng

Pass
hu zhao

Transport

jiao tong yun shu

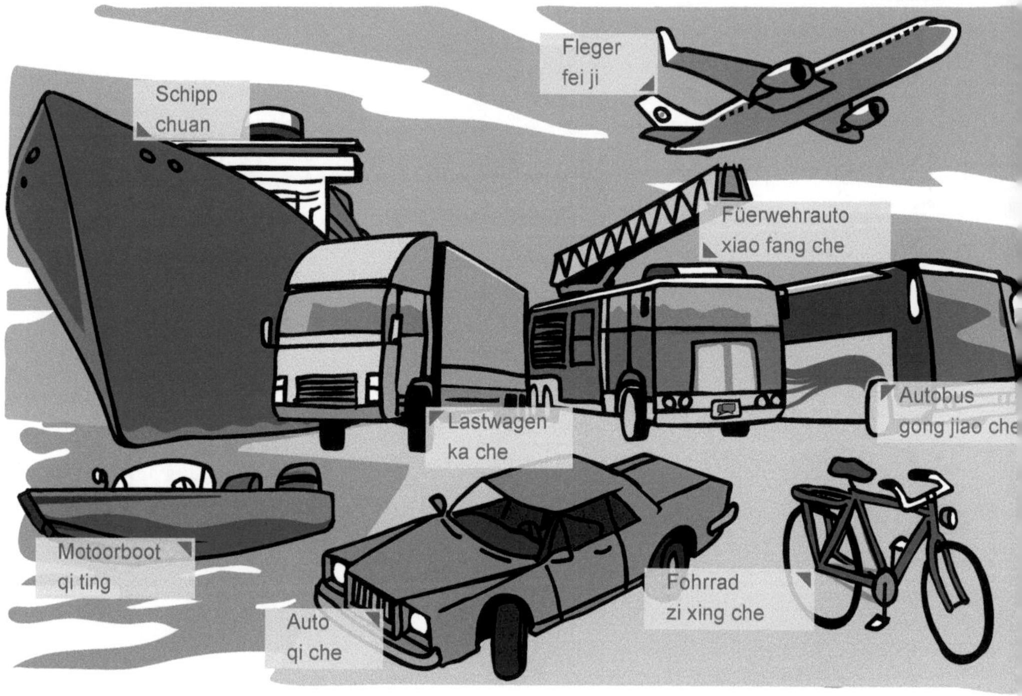

Fleger
fei ji
Schipp
chuan
Füerwehrauto
xiao fang che
Autobus
gong jiao che
Lastwagen
ka che
Motoorboot
qi ting
Fohrrad
zi xing che
Auto
qi che

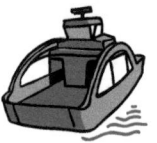

Fähr

bai du chuan

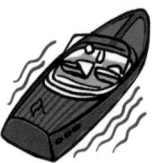

Boot

xiao chuan

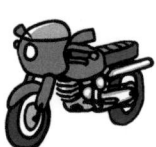

Motoorrad

mo tuo che

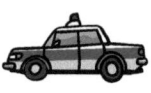

Polizeiauto

jing che

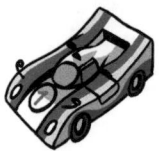

Rönnauto

sai che

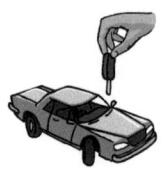

Lehnwagen

zu che

Carsharing

pin che

Afsleepwagen

tuo che

Müllauto

la ji che

Motoor

fa dong ji

Kraftstoff

qi you

Tanksteed

jia you zhan

Verkehrsschild

jiao tong biao zhi

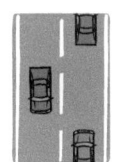

Verkehr

jiao tong

Stau

jiao tong du sai

Afstellplatz

ting che chang

Bahnhoff

huo che zhan

Sporen

gui dao

Tog

huo che

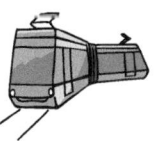

Stratenbahn

dian che

Wagon

huo che

Dwarsmöhl

zhi sheng ji

Flooghaven

ji chang

Tower

ta

Fohrgast

cheng ke

Grootkist

ji zhuang xiang

Karton

zhi ban xiang

Koor

shou tui che

Korf

lan zi

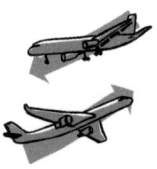

starten / lannen

qi fei/jiang luo

Stadt

cheng shi

Dörp

cun zhuang

Binnenstadt

shi zhong xin

Huus

fang zi

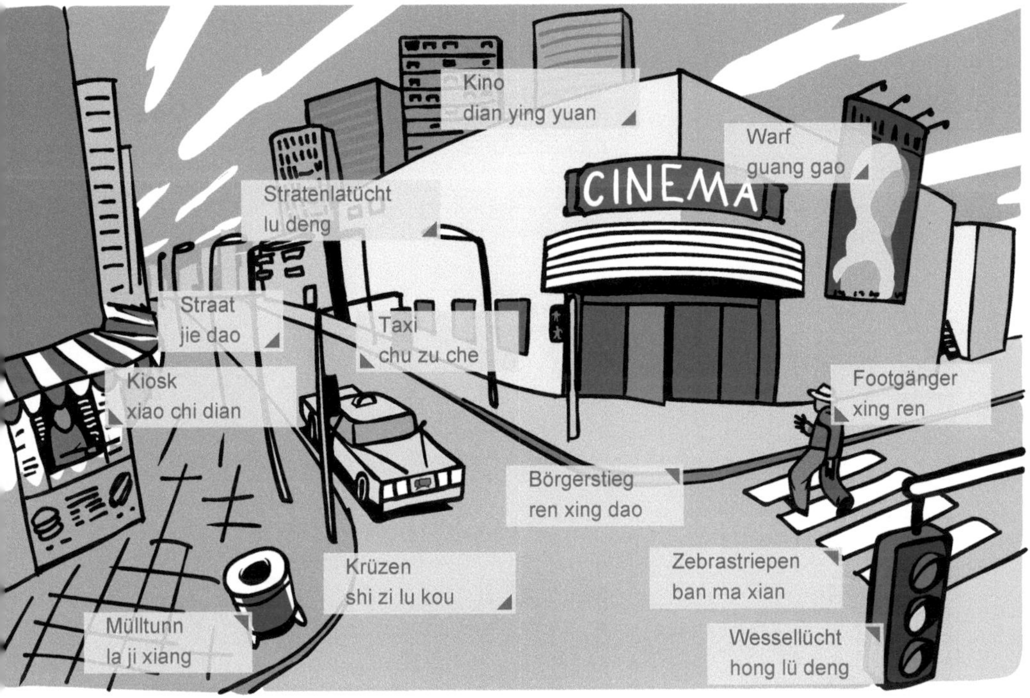

CINEMA
Kino
dian ying yuan
Warf
guang gao
Stratenlatücht
lu deng
Straat
jie dao
Taxi
chu zu che
Kiosk
xiao chi dian
Footgänger
xing ren
Börgerstieg
ren xing dao
Krüzen
shi zi lu kou
Zebrastriepen
ban ma xian
Mülltunn
la ji xiang
Wessellücht
hong lü deng

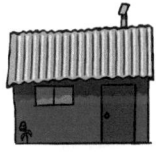

Hütt

xiao wu

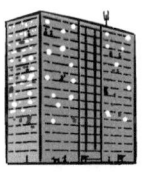

Wahnung

gong yu

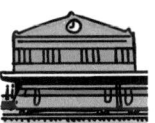

Bahnhoff

huo che zhan

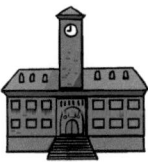

Raathuus

shi zheng ting

MUSEUM

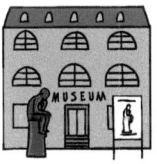

Museum

bo wu guan

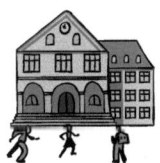

School

xue xiao

Universität

da xue

Bank

yin hang

Krankenhuus

yi yuan

Hotel

jiu dian

Afteek

yao fang

Büro

ban gong shi

Bookhökerie

shu dian

Hökerie

shang dian

Blomenhökerie

hua dian

Supermarkt

chao shi

Markt

shi chang

Koophuus

bai huo shang dian

Fischhökerie

yu dian

Inkoopszentrum

gou wu zhong xin

Haven

hai gang

Parkanlaag

gong yuan

Bank

chang deng

Brüch

qiao

Trepp

lou ti

Ünnergrundbahn

di tie

Tunnel

sui dao

Busstoppsteed

gong jiao che zhan

Bar

jiu ba

Spieslokal

can guan

Breefkassen

you tong

Stratenschild

lu biao

Parkklock

ting che ji shi qi

Deertenpark

dong wu yuan

Baadanstalt

you yong guan

Moschee

qing zhen si

Buernhoff

nong chang

Ümweltversmudden

wu ran

Karkhoff

mu di

Kark

jiao tang

Speelplatz

cao chang

Tempel

si miao

Landschop

di xing

Blatt
shu ye

Wiespahl
zhi shi pai

Weg
lu

Wisch
cao di

Steen
shi tou

Boom
shu

Wannerer
tu bu lü xing zhe

Fluss
he

Gras
cao

Bloom
hua

Daal

xia gu

Barg

shan

See

hu

Holt

sen lin

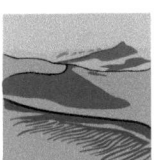

Wööst

sha mo

Füerspien Barg

huo shan

Slott

cheng bao

Regenbagen

cai hong

Poggenstohl

mo gu

Palm

zong lü shu

Steekmück

wen zi

Fleeg

cang ying

Miegeemk

ma yi

Imm

mi feng

Spinn

zhi zhu

Sebber

jia chong

Pogg

qing wa

Katteker

song shu

Swienegel

ci wei

Haas

ye tu

Uul

mao tou ying

Vagel

niao

Swaan

tian e

Wildswien

ye zhu

Hirsch

lu

Elk

mi lu

Staudamm

shui ba

Windrad

feng li fa dian ji

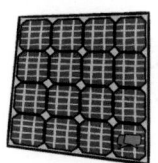

Solarmodul

tai yang neng dian chi ban

Klima

qi hou

Spieslokal
can guan

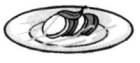

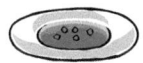

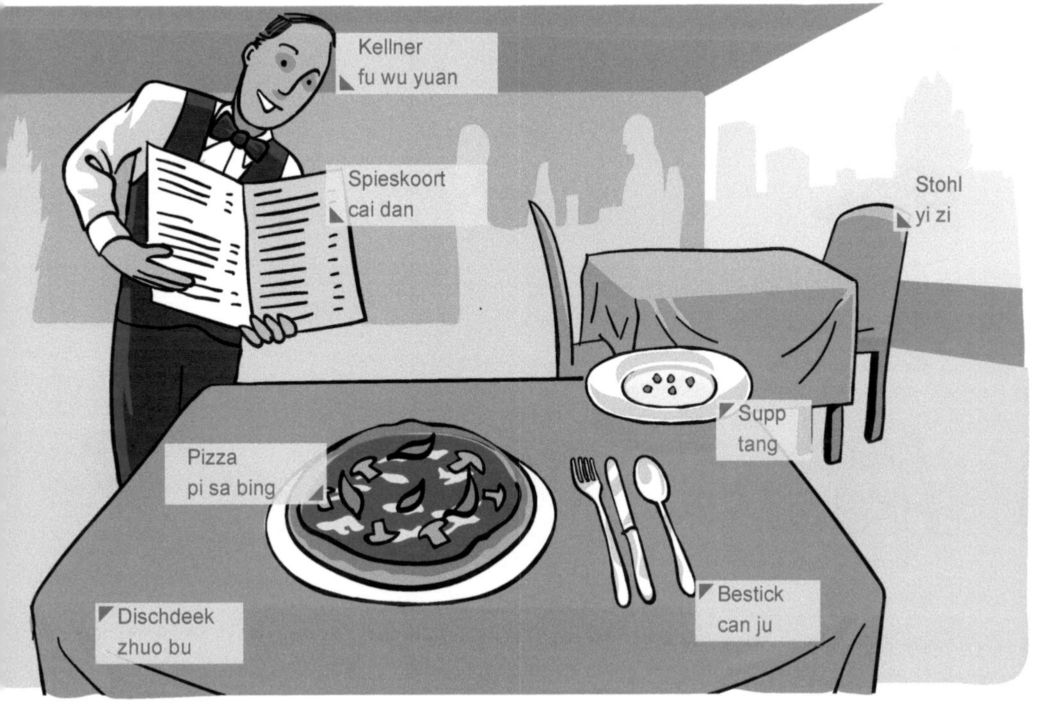
Kellner
fu wu yuan
Spieskoort
cai dan
Stohl
yi zi
Supp
tang
Pizza
pi sa bing
Bestick
can ju
Dischdeek
zhuo bu

Vörspies

qian cai

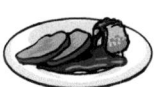

Haupteten

zhu cai

Nadisch

tian dian

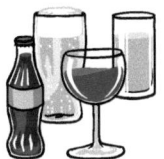

Drünk

yin liao

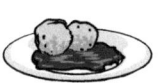

Eten

shi wu

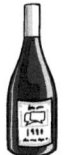

Buddel

ping zi

Fastfood

kuai can

Strateneten

jie bian xiao chi

Teekann

cha hu

Zuckerdoos

tang he

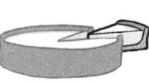

Portschoon

yi fen fan cai

Espressomaschien

yi shi ka fei ji

Hoochstohl

gao jiao yi

Reken

zhang dan

Tablett

tuo pan

Mess

dao

Gavel

can cha

Lepel

shao zi

Teelepel

cha chi

Munddook

can jin

Glas

bo li bei

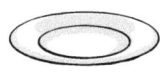

Töller

die zi

Suppentöller

tang pan

Ünnertass

die zi

Sooß

jiang

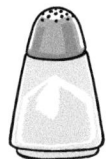

Soltstreuer

yan ping

Pepermöhl

hu jiao mo

Etig

cu

Ööl

shi yong you

Krüder

tiao wei liao

Ketchup

fan qie jiang

Mostrich

jie mo

Mayonnaise

dan huang jiang

Supermarkt

chao shi

Anbott
te jia
FOR
Kunn
gu ke
Melkprodukten
ru zhi pin
Aaft
shui guo
Inkoopswagen
gou wu che

BUTCHERS

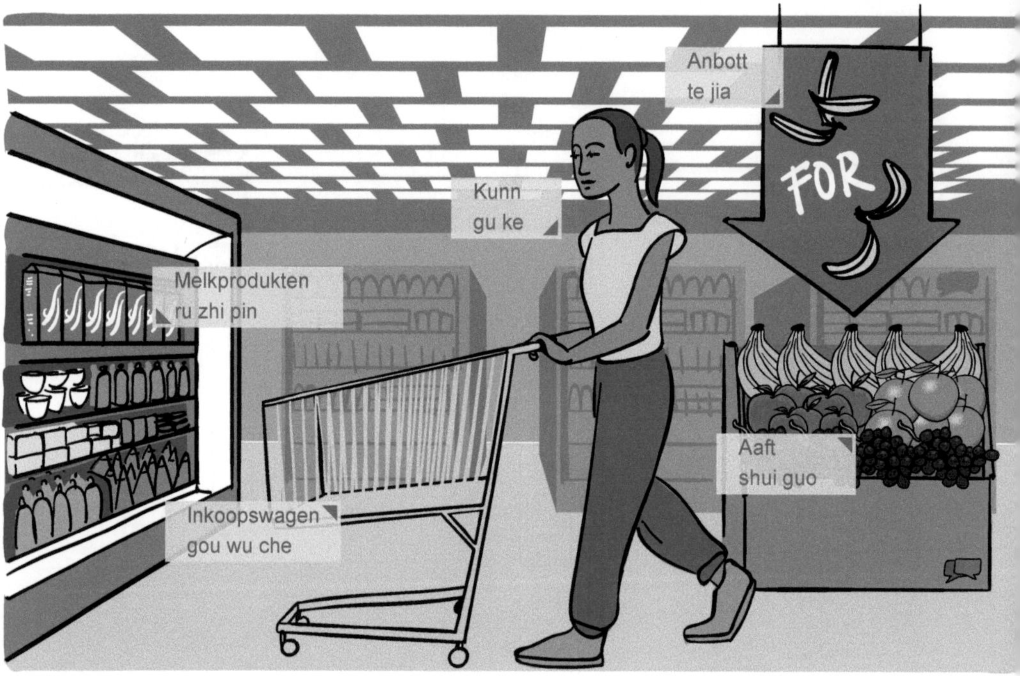

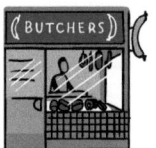

Slachterie

rou pu

BAKERY

Bäckerie

mian bao fang

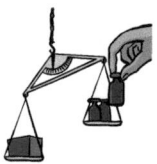

wegen

cheng zhong

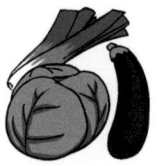

Gröönsaken

shu cai

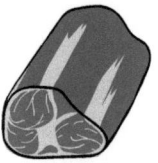

Fleesch

rou

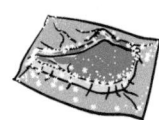

Deepköhlkost

leng dong shi pin

Opsnitt

leng pan

Konserven

guan tou shi pin

Waschmiddel

xi yi fen

Snoopkraam

tian shi

Huushooltssaken

ri yong pin

Reinmaaktüüch

qing jie yong pin

Verköpersche

xiao shou yuan

Kass

shou yin ji

Kasserer

shou yin yuan

Inkoopslist

gou wu qing dan

Opsparrtieden

kai fang shi jian

Breeftasch

qian bao

Kreditkoort

xin yong ka

Tasch

dai zi

Plastiktüüt

su liao dai

Drünk

yin liao

Water

shui

Saft

guo zhi

Melk

niu nai

Cola

ke le

Wien

hong jiu

Beer

pi jiu

Spriet

jiu

Kakao

ke ke

Tee

cha

Koffie

ka fei

Espresso

yi shi nong suo ka fei

Cappucino

ka bu qi nuo

Banaan

xiang jiao

Appel

ping guo

Appelsien

cheng zi

Meloon

xi gua

Zitroon

ning meng

Wöttel

hu luo bo

Knuuvlook

da suan

Bambus

zhu zi

Zibbel

yang cong

Poggenstohl

mo gu

Nööt

jian guo

Nudeln

mian tiao

Spaghetti

yi da li mian tiao

Ries

mi fan

Salat

sha la

Pommes frites

shu tiao

Braadkantüffeln

zha tu dou

Pizza

pi sa bing

Hamborger

han bao bao

Sandwich

san ming zhi

Snitzel

zha zhu pai

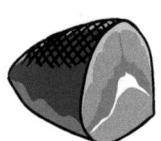

Schinken

huo tui

Salami

sa la mi

Wust

xiang chang

Hohn

ji rou

Braden

kao rou

Fisch

yu

Haverflocken

yan mai pian

Müsli

mu zi li

Cornflakes

yu mi pian

Mehl

mian fen

Croissant

yang jiao mian bao

Rundstück

mian bao juan

Broot

mian bao

Toast

kao mian bao

Keksen

bing gan

Botter

huang you

Quark

ning ru

Koken

dan gao

Ei

dan

Spegelei

jian dan

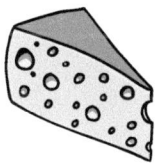

Kees

nai lao

Ies
bing ji lin

Zucker
tang

Honnig
feng mi

Marmelaad
guo jiang

Nougat-Creme
qiao ke li jiang

Curry
ga li fan

Buernhoff
nong chang

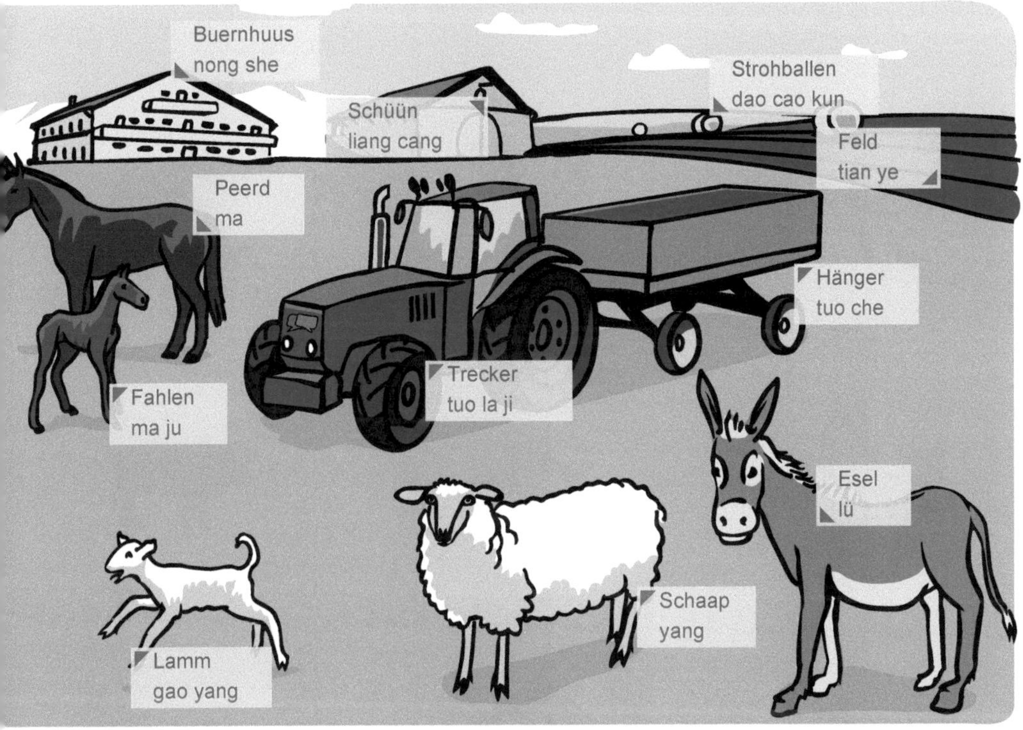
Buernhuus
nong she
Schüün
liang cang
Strohballen
dao cao kun
Feld
tian ye
Peerd
ma
Hänger
tuo che
Trecker
tuo la ji
Fahlen
ma ju
Esel
lü
Schaap
yang
Lamm
gao yang

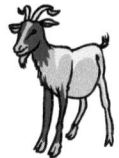

Zeeg

shan yang

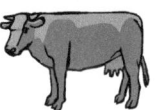

Koh

nai niu

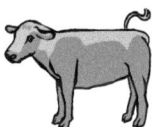

Kalf

niu du

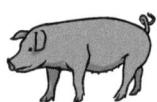

Swien

zhu

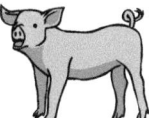

Farken

xiao zhu

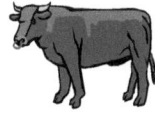

Bull

gong niu

Goos

e

Aant

ya

Küken

xiao ji

Hohn

mu ji

Hahn

gong ji

Rott

shu

Katt

mao

Muus

lao shu

Oss

niu

Hund

gou

Hunnenhütt

gou wu

Goornslauch

hua yuan jiao shui ruan
guan

Geetkann

sa shui hu

Lee

chang bing da lian dao

Ploog

li

Sich

lian dao

Hack

chu tou

Mestfork

chang bing cao pa

Ext

fu tou

Schuufkoor

du lun shou tui che

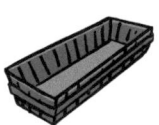

Trog

si liao cao

Melkkann

niu nai guan

Sack

ma bu dai

Tuun

zha lan

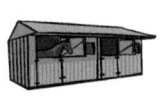

Stall

ma jiu

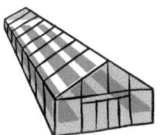

Drievhuus

wen shi

Bodden

tu rang

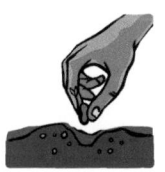

Saat

zhong zi

Dünger

fei liao

Meihdöscher

lian he shou ge ji

oornen

shou ge

Oorn

shou ge

Yamswöttel

shan yao

Weten

xiao mai

Soja

da dou

Kantüffel

tu dou

Törksche Weten

yu mi

Rapp

you cai zi

Aaftboom

guo shu

Troopsch Kantüffel

shu shu

Koorn

gu wu

Huus

fang zi

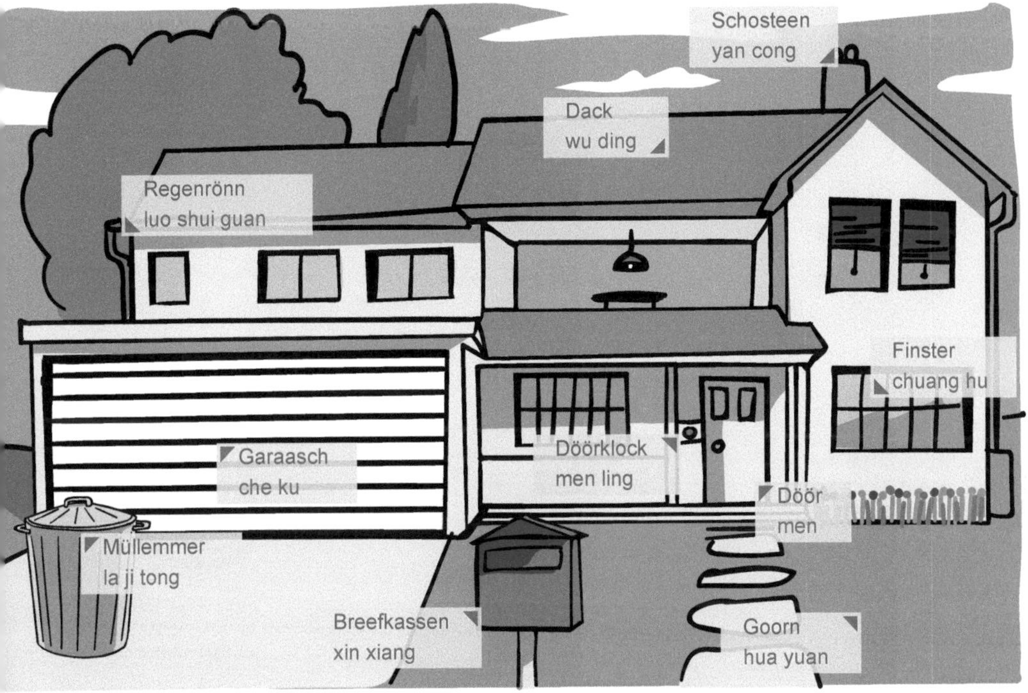

Schosteen
yan cong
Dack
wu ding
Regenrönn
luo shui guan
Finster
chuang hu
Garaasch
che ku
Döörklock
men ling
Döör
men
Müllemmer
la ji tong
Breefkassen
xin xiang
Goorn
hua yuan

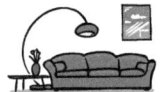

Wahnstuuv

ke ting

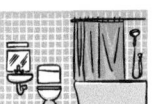

Baadstuuv

yu shi

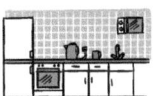

Köök

chu fang

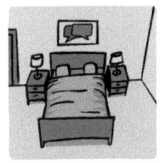

Slaapstuuv

wo shi

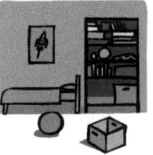

Kinnerstuuv

er tong fang

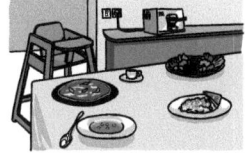

Eetstuuv

can ting

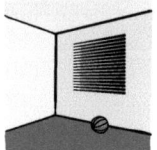

Footbodden

di ban

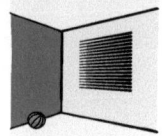

Wand

qiang bi

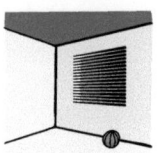

Deek

diao ding

Keller

di jiao

Hittluftbad

sang na

Balkon

yang tai

Terrass

lu tai

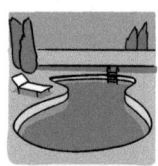

Swümmbad

you yong chi

Rasenmeiher

ge cao ji

Bettbetog

bei dan

Bettdeek

chuang zhao

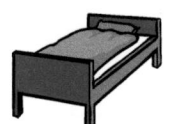

Puuch

chuang

Bessen

sao zhou

Emmer

shui tong

Schalter

kai guan

Wahnstuuv

ke ting

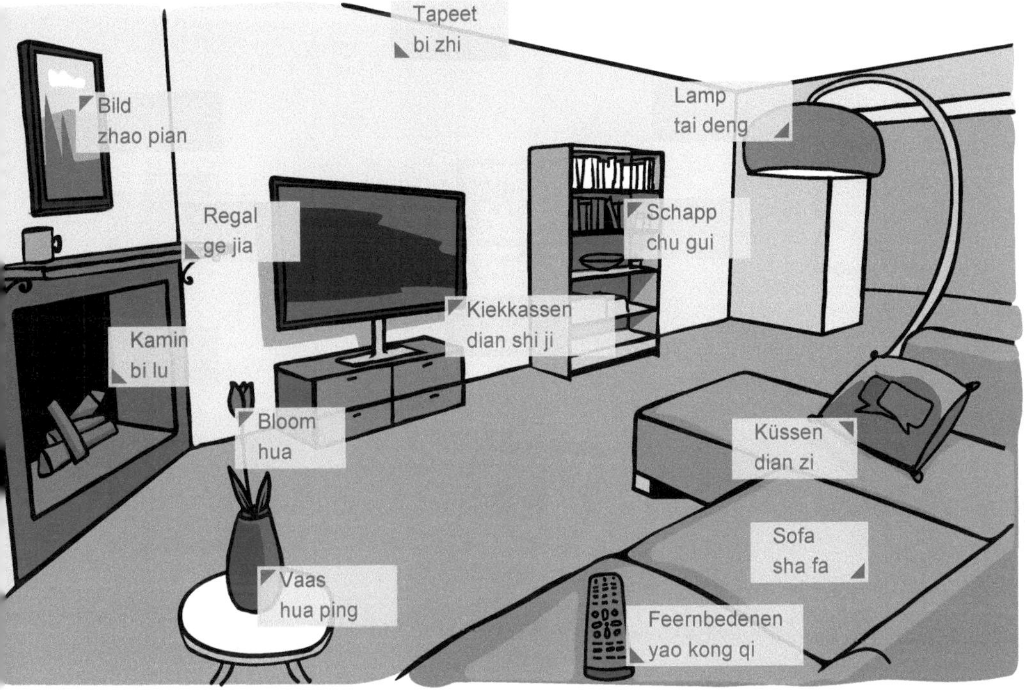
Tapeet
bi zhi
Bild
zhao pian
Lamp
tai deng
Regal
ge jia
Schapp
chu gui
Kiekkassen
dian shi ji
Kamin
bi lu
Bloom
hua
Küssen
dian zi
Sofa
sha fa
Vaas
hua ping
Feernbedenen
yao kong qi

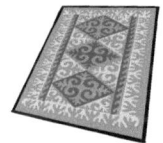

Teppich

di tan

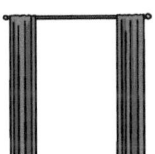

Vörhang

chuang lian

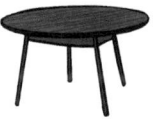

Disch

can zhuo

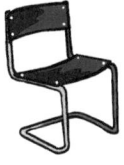

Stohl

yi zi

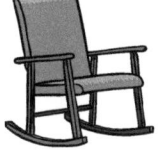

Schuckelstohl

yao yi

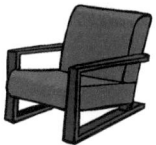

Sessel

fu shou yi

Book

shu

Deek

tan zi

Dekoratschoon

zhuang shi pin

Füerholt

mu chai

Film

dian ying

Stereoanlaag

gao bao zhen yin xiang

Slötel

yao shi

Narichtenblatt

bao zhi

Gemälde

you hua

Poster

hai bao

Radio

shou yin ji

Opschrievblock

bi ji ben

Huulbessen

xi chen qi

Kaktus

xian ren zhang

Kars

la zhu

Köök
chu fang

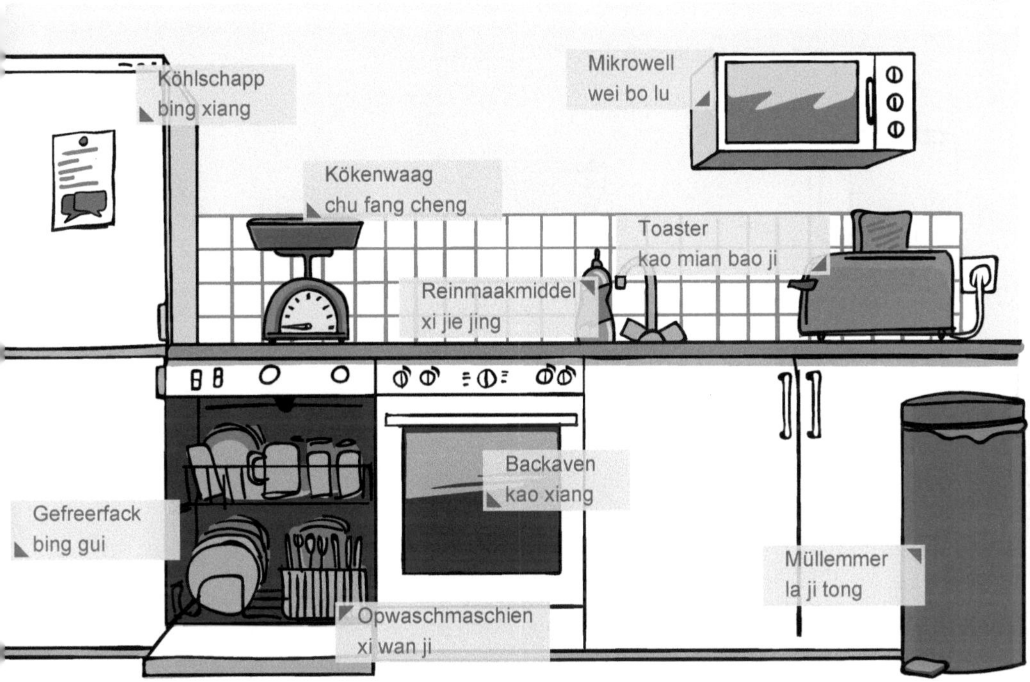

Köhlschapp
bing xiang
Mikrowell
wei bo lu
Kökenwaag
chu fang cheng
Toaster
kao mian bao ji
Reinmaakmiddel
xi jie jing
Backaven
kao xiang
Gefreerfack
bing gui
Müllemmer
la ji tong
Opwaschmaschien
xi wan ji

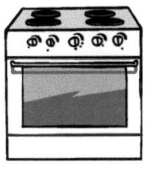

Heerd

chui ju

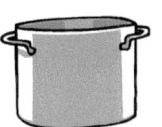

Pott

guo

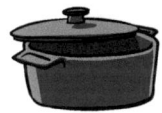

Gussiesern Putt

zhu tie guo

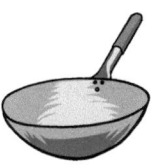

Wok / Kadai

sha guo

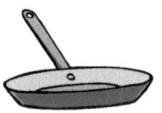

Pann

ping di guo

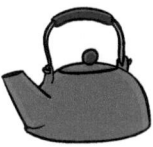

Waterkaker

shui hu

Dampkaakputt

zheng guo

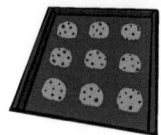

Backblick

kao pan

Geschirr

tao ci guo

Beker

ma ke bei

Schaal

wan

Eetsticken

kuai zi

Suppenkell

chang bing shao

Pannenwenner

chan zi

Sneebessen

jiao ban qi

Kaakseef

lü wang

Seef

shai zi

Riev

mo sui ji

Mörser

yan bo

Grill

shao kao

Füerstell

ming huo

Sniedbrett

cai ban

Nudelholt

gan mian zhang

Proppentrecker

kai ping qi

Doos

guan zi

Dosenaapner

kai ping qi

Pottlappen

ge re shou tao

Waschbecken

shui cao

Böst

shua zi

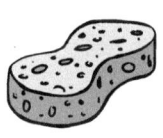

Swamm

hai mian

Mixer

jiao ban ji

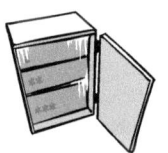

Iesschapp

leng cang xiang

Nuckelbuddel

nai ping

Waterhahn

shui long tou

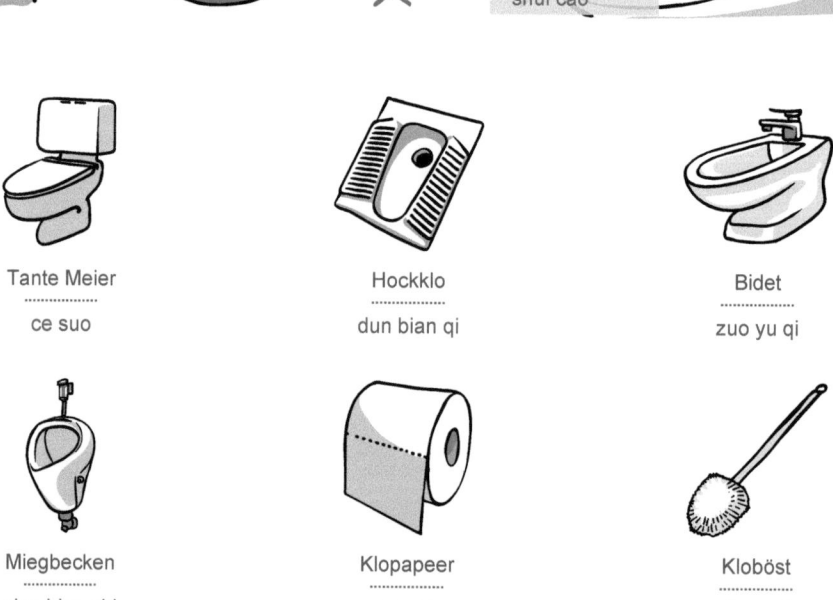

Baadstuuv

yu shi

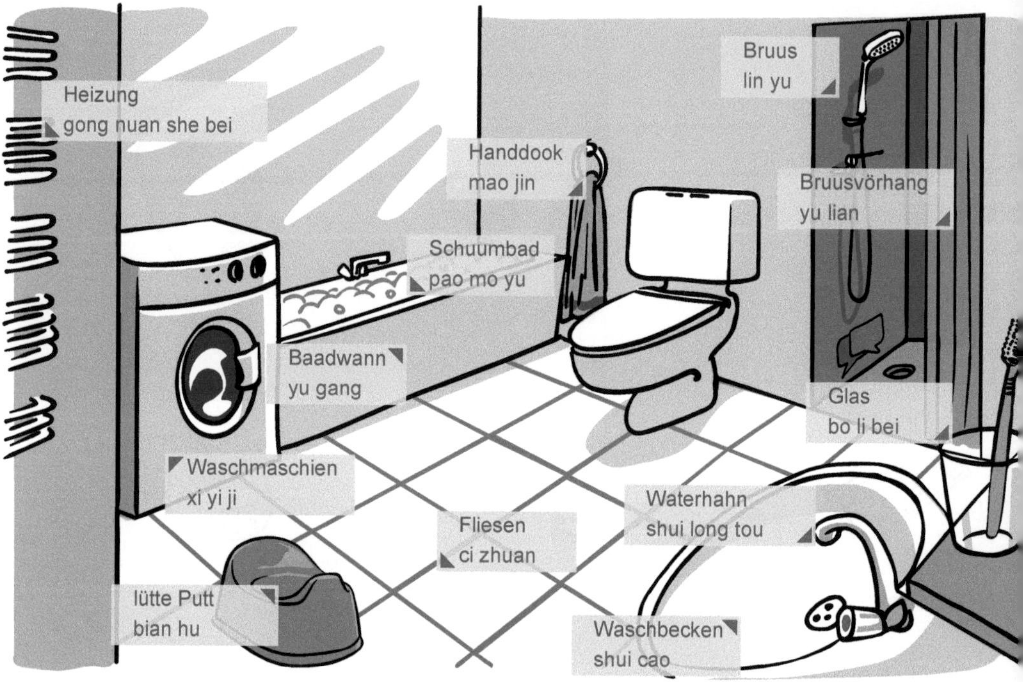

Heizung
gong nuan she bei
Handdook
mao jin
Bruus
lin yu
Bruusvörhang
yu lian
Schuumbad
pao mo yu
Baadwann
yu gang
Glas
bo li bei
Waschmaschien
xi yi ji
Waterhahn
shui long tou
Fliesen
ci zhuan
lütte Putt
bian hu
Waschbecken
shui cao

Tante Meier

ce suo

Hockklo

dun bian qi

Bidet

zuo yu qi

Miegbecken

xiao bian chi

Klopapeer

ce zhi

Kloböst

ma tong shua

Tähnböst

ya shua

Tähnpast

ya gao

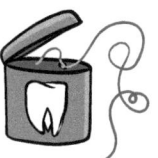

Tähnsied

ya xian

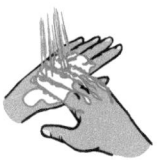

waschen

xi

Handbruus

shou chi shi pen lin tou

Intimbruus

chong xi qi

Waschschöttel

xi lian pen

Rüchböst

ca bei shua

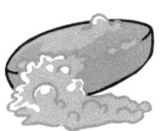

Seep

fei zao

Bruusgeel

mu yu lu

Hoorwaschmiddel

xi fa shui

Waschlappen

fa lan rong

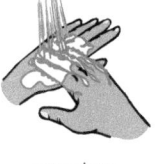

Afloop

pai shui

Creme

ru shuang

Deodorant

chu chou ji

Spegel

jing zi

Kosmetikspegel

shou jing

Raserer

ti xu dao

Raseerschuum

ti xu pao mo

Raseerwater

xu hou shui

Kamm

shu zi

Böst

shua zi

Hoordröger

chui feng ji

Hoorspray

pen fa ding xing ji

Smink

hua zhuang pin

Lippensticken

chun gao

Nagellack

zhi jia you

Watt

hua zhuang mian

Nagelscheer

zhi jia jian

Rüükwater

xiang shui

Kulturbüdel

xi shu bao

Schemel

deng zi

Waag

ji zhong cheng

Baadmantel

yu pao

Gummihanschen

xiang jiao shou tao

Tampon

wei sheng mian tiao

Damenbinn

wei sheng jin

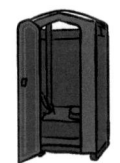

Chemieklo

hua xue ce suo

Kinnerstuuv

er tong fang

Wecker
nao zhong
Knudeldeert
mao rong wan ju
Speeltüüchauto
wan ju che
Klöter
bo lang gu
Poppenhuus
wan ju wu
Geschenk
li wu

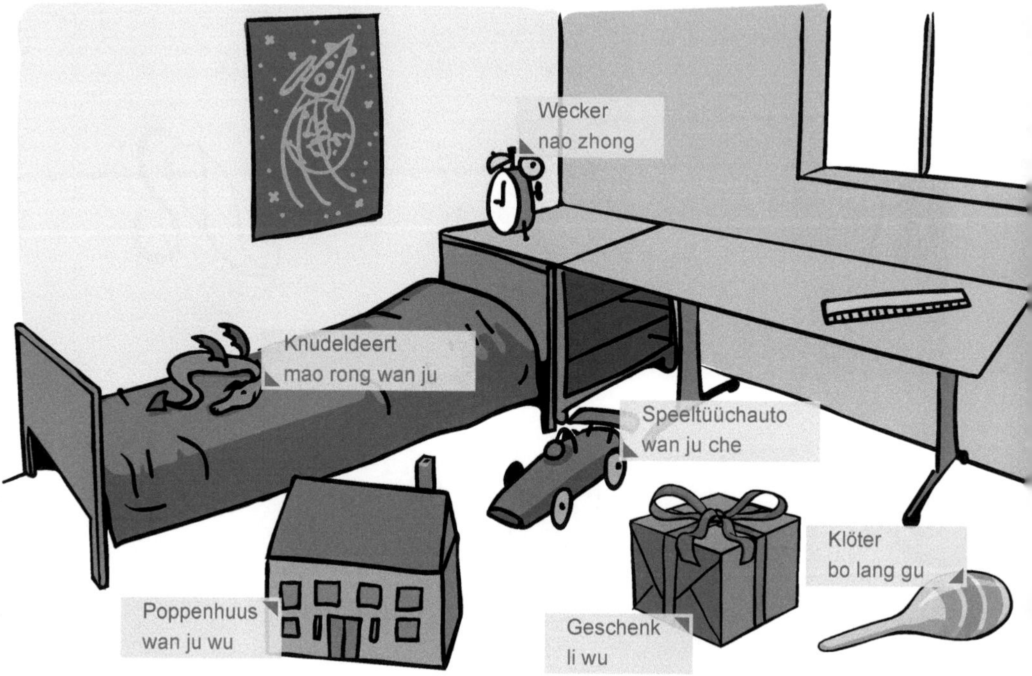

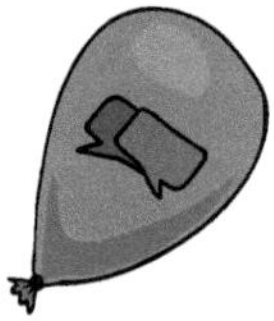

Luftballon

qi qiu

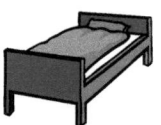

Puuch

chuang

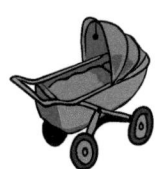

Kinnerwagen

(yang wa wa yong)ying er che

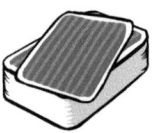

Koortenspeel

pu ke pai

Puzzle

pin tu

SUPER MEGA

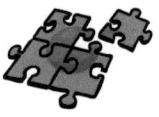

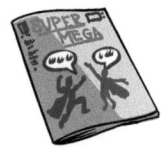

Billergeschicht

man hua

Legostenen

le gao ji mu

Bustenen

ji mu wan ju

Action-Figur

wan ju ren

Strampelantog

ying er fu

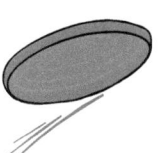

Frisbeeschiev

fei pan

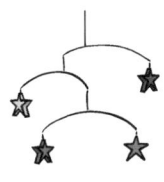

Mobile

chuang ling wan ju

Brettspeel

qi pan you xi

Wörpel

shai zi

Modelliesenbahn

huo che mo xing

Snuller

an fu nai zui

Party

ju hui

Billerbook

hui ben

Ball

qiu

Popp

yang wa wa

spelen

wan

Sandkassen

sha keng

Schuckel

qiu qian

Speeltüüch

wan ju

Speelkonsool

you xi ji

Dreerad

san lun che

Teddyboor

tai di xiong

Klederschapp

yi chu

Tüüch

yi fu

Socken

wa zi

Strümp

chang wa

Strumpbüx

jin shen ku

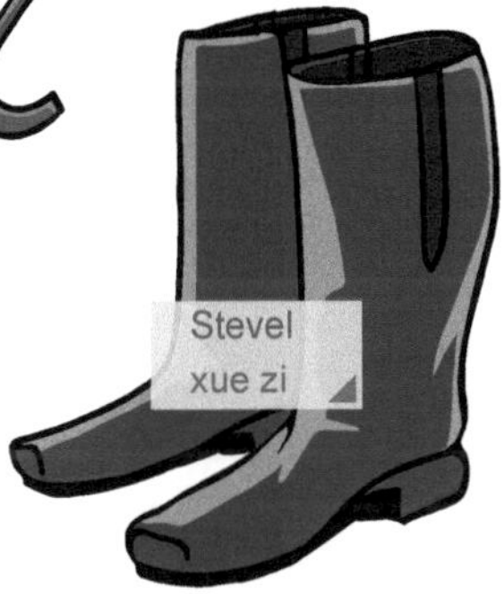

Halsdook
wei jin

Paraplü
yu san

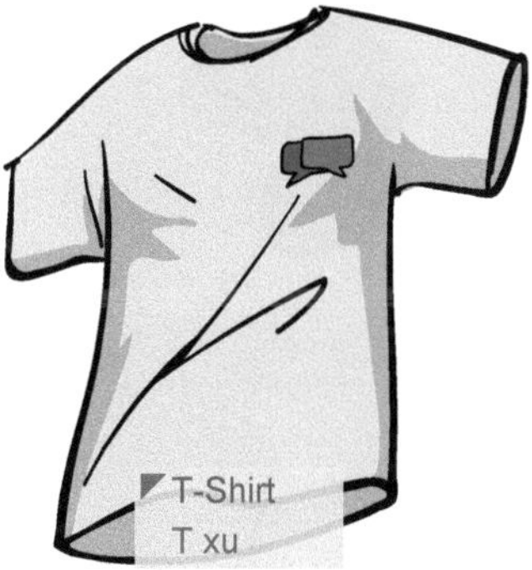

T-Shirt
T xu

Liefreem
pi dai

Stevel
xue zi

Puuschen
tuo xie

Turnschoh
yun dong xie

Sandalen
liang xie

Schoh
xie

Gummistevel
yu xue

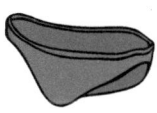

Ünnerbüx
nei ku

Bostholler
xiong zhao

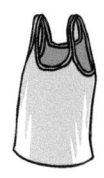

Ünnerhemd
bei xin

Lief

shen ti

Büx

ku zi

Jeansnüx

niu zai ku

Rock

duan qun

Bluus

nü shi chen shan

Hemd

chen shan

Pullover

tao tou shan

Kapuzenpullover

wei yi

Blazer

xi zhuang jia ke

Jack

jia ke

Mantel

wai tao

Övertrecker

yu yi

Kostüm

tao zhuang

Kleed

lian yi qun

Hochtietskleed

hun sha

Antog

xi zhuang

Nachtkleed

shui pao

Slaapantog

shui yi

Sari

sha li

Koppdook

tou jin

Turban

bao tou jin

Burka

bo ka

Kaftan

ka fu tan

Abaya

(a la bo shi)chang pao

Baadantog

yong yi

Baadbüx

nan shi yong ku

Korte Büx

duan ku

Antog to'n Öven

yun dong fu

Schört

wei qun

Handschoh

shou tao

Knopp

niu kou

Brill

yan jing

Armband

shou lian

Halskeed

xiang lian

Ring

jie zhi

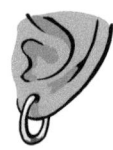

Ohrbummel

er huan

Mütz

bian mao

Klederbögel

yi jia

Hoot

mao zi

Binner

ling dai

Rietslüter

la lian

Helm

tou kui

Drachtband

bei dai

Schooluniform

xiao fu

Uniform

zhi fu

Severbölen
....
wei dou

Snuller
....
an fu nai zui

Winnel
....
niao bu shi

Büro

ban gong shi

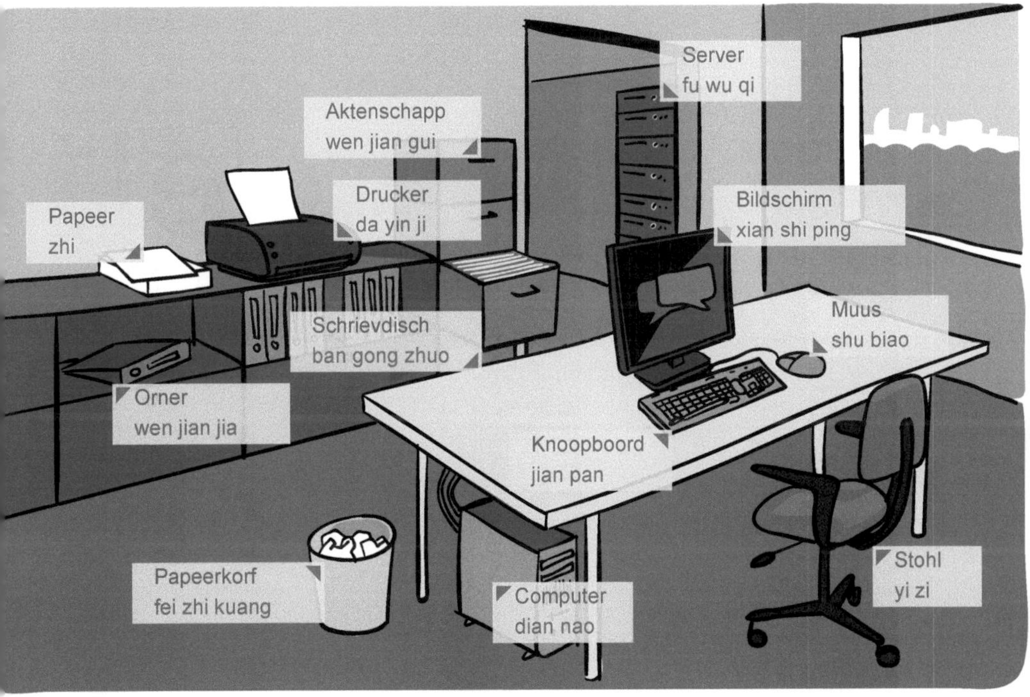

Server
fu wu qi

Aktenschapp
wen jian gui

Drucker
da yin ji

Bildschirm
xian shi ping

Papeer
zhi

Muus
shu biao

Schrievdisch
ban gong zhuo

Orner
wen jian jia

Knoopboord
jian pan

Papeerkorf
fei zhi kuang

Stohl
yi zi

Computer
dian nao

Koffiebeker
....
ka fei bei

Taschenreekner
....
ji suan qi

Internet
....
yin te wang

Klappreekner

bi ji ben dian nao

Breef

xin jian

Naricht

xiao xi

Ackersnacker

shou ji

Nettwark

wang luo

Kopeerapparat

fu yin ji

Software

ruan jian

Klöönkassen

dian hua

Steekdoos

cha zuo

Faxapparat

chuan zhen ji

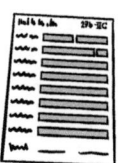

Formulor

biao ge

Dokument

wen jian

köpen

mai

betahlen

fu qian

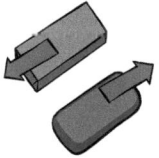

hanneln

jiao yi

Geld

xian jin

Dollar

mei yuan

Euro

ou yuan

Yen

ri yuan

Ruvel

lu bu

Swiezer Franken

rui shi fa lang

Renminbi Yuan

ren min bi

Rupie

lu bi

Geldautomat

ti kuan chu

Wesselstuuv

wai bi dui huan chu

Gold

jin

Sülver

yin

Ööl

shi you

Energie

neng yuan

Pries

jia ge

Verdrag

he tong

Stüer

shui jin

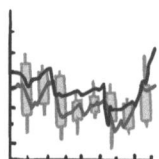

Andeelschien

gu piao

arbeiden

gong zuo

Anstellte

zhi yuan

Arbeitgever

lao ban

Fabrik

gong chang

Hökerie

shang dian

Profeschonen
zhi ye

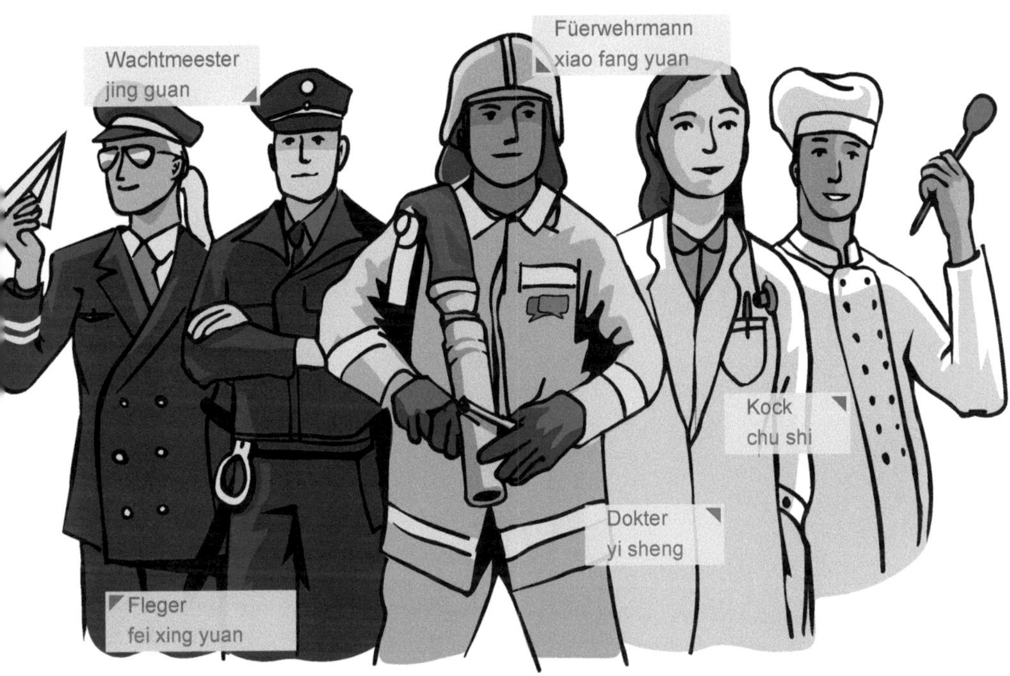

Wachtmeester
jing guan
Füerwehrmann
xiao fang yuan
Kock
chu shi
Dokter
yi sheng
Fleger
fei xing yuan

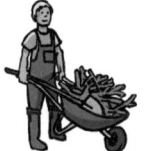

Goorner

yuan ding

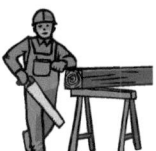

Discher

mu jiang

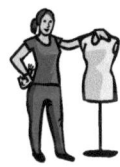

Neihersche

cai feng

Richter

fa guan

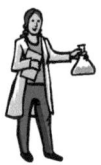

Chemiker

hua xue jia

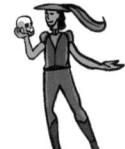

Schauspeler

yan yuan

Busfohrer

gong jiao che si ji

Taxifohrer

chu zu che si ji

Fischer

yu fu

Reinmaakfru

qing jie nü gong

Dackdecker

wu ding gong

Kellner

fu wu yuan

Jäger

lie ren

Maler

hua jia

Bäcker

mian bao shi

Elektriker

dian gong

Buarbeider

jian zhu gong ren

Ingenieur

gong cheng shi

Slachter

tu fu

Klempner

shui guan gong

Postbüdel

you di yuan

Suldat

shi bing

Architekt

jian zhu shi

Kasserer

shou yin yuan

Florist

hua nong

Putzbüdel

li fa shi

Schaffner

shou piao yuan

Mechaniker

ji xie shi

Kaptein

chuan zhang

Tähndokter

ya yi

Wetenschopler

ke xue jia

Rabbi

la bi

Imam

yi ma mu

Mönk

he shang

Paap

mu shi

Warktüüch

gong ju

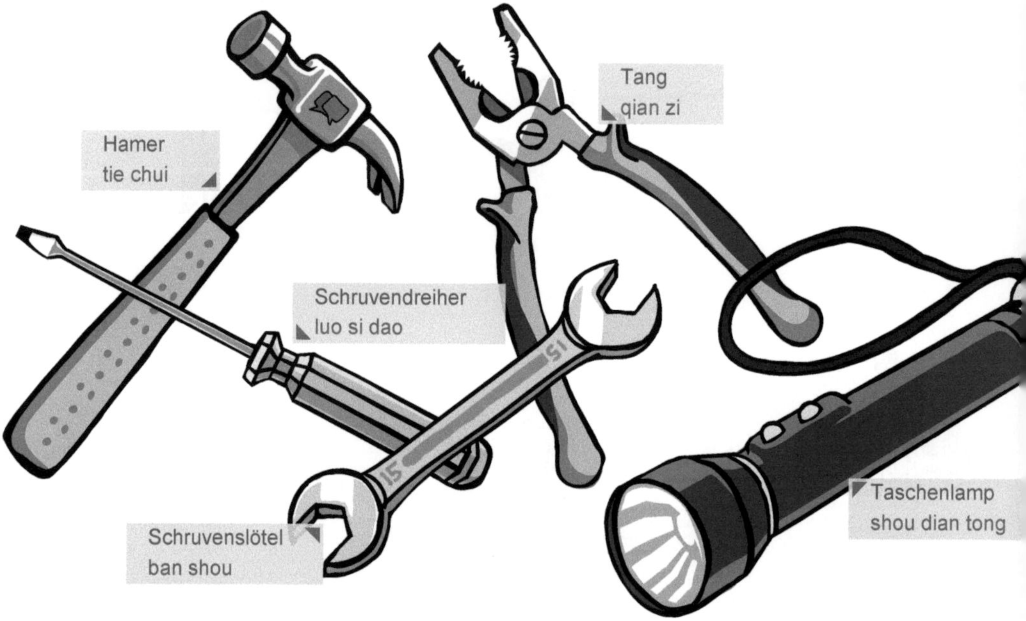

Tang
qian zi
Hamer
tie chui
Schruvendreiher
luo si dao
Taschenlamp
shou dian tong
Schruvenslötel
ban shou

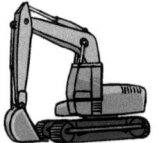

Grieper

wa jue ji

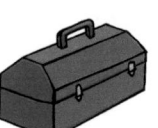

Warktüüchkassen

gong ju xiang

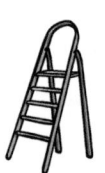

Ledder

ti zi

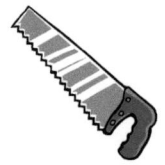

Saag

ju zi

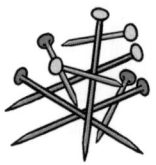

Nagels

ding zi

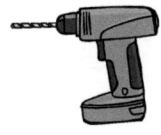

Bohrer

zuan ji

heelmaken
xiu

Schüffel
chan zi

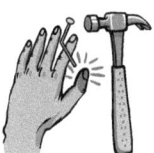

Schiet!
kao!

Kehrblick
bo ji

Farvpott
you qi tong

Schruven
luo si

Musikinstrumenten
yue qi

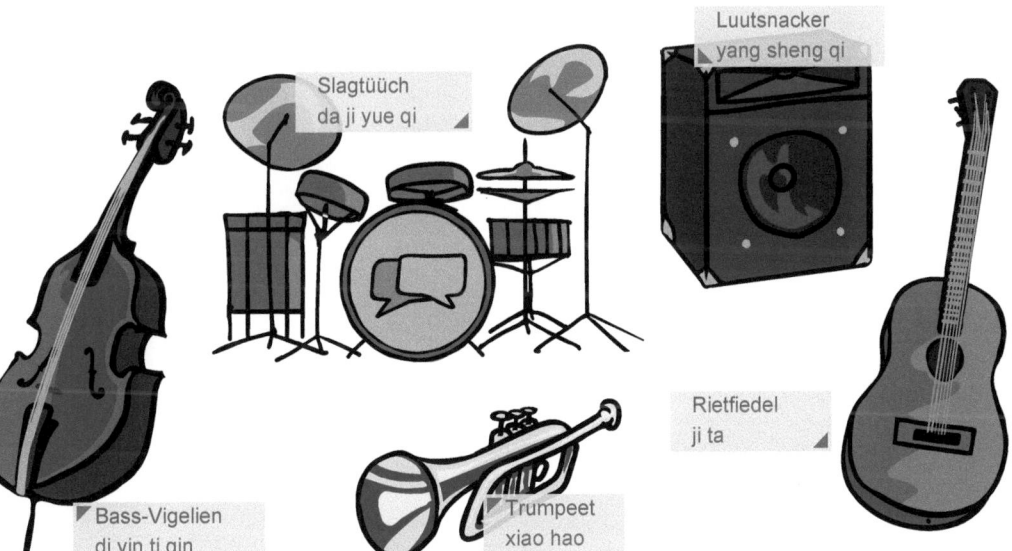

Luutsnacker
yang sheng qi

Slagtüüch
da ji yue qi

Bass-Vigelien
di yin ti qin

Trumpeet
xiao hao

Rietfiedel
ji ta

Klaveer

gang qin

Vigelien

xiao ti qin

Bass

bei si

Pauk

ding yin gu

Trummeln

gu

Keyboard

dian zi qin

Saxophon

sa ke si guan

Fleut

chang di

Mikrofoon

mai ke feng

Deertenpark

dong wu yuan

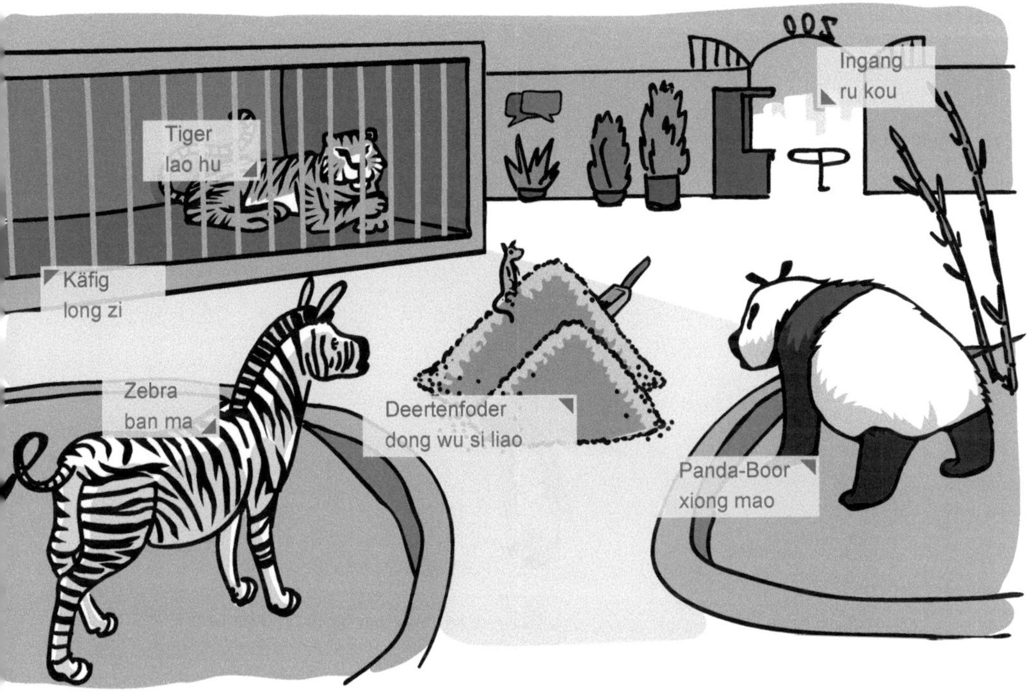

Ingang
ru kou
Tiger
lao hu
Käfig
long zi
Zebra
ban ma
Deertenfoder
dong wu si liao
Panda-Boor
xiong mao

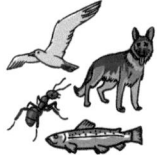

Deerten

dong wu

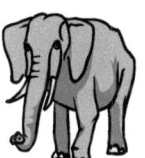

Elefant

da xiang

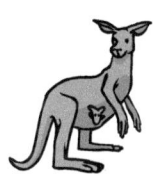

Känguru

dai shu

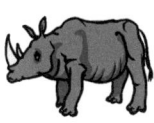

Neeshoorn

xi niu

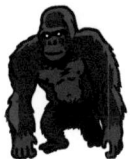

Gorilla

da xing xing

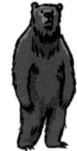

Boor

xiong

Kameel

luo tuo

Struuß

tuo niao

Lööv

shi zi

Aap

hou zi

Flamingo

huo lie niao

Papagoi

ying wu

lesboor

bei ji xiong

Pinguin

qi e

Haifisch

sha yu

Pageluun

kong que

Slang

she

Krokodil

e yu

Oppasser in'n Deertenpark

dong wu yuan guan li yuan

Saalhund

hai bao

Jaguor

mei zhou bao

Pony

ai zhong ma

Leopard

bao

Nilpeerd

he ma

Giraff

chang jing lu

Aadler

lao ying

Wildswien

ye zhu

Fisch

yu

Schildkrööt

gui

Walross

hai xiang

Voss

hu li

Gazell

ling yang

Amerikaansch Football
gan lan qiu

Radfohren
qi zi xing che

Tennis
wang qiu

Korfball
lan qiu

Swümmen
you yong

Boxen
quan ji

Ieshockey
bing qiu

Football
ying shi zu qiu

Fedderball
yu mao qiu

Leichtathletik
tian jing

Handball
shou qiu

Skilopen
hua xue

Polo
ma qiu

Aktivitäten
huo dong

lachen
xiao
springen
tiao
ümarmen
yong bao
gahn
zou lu
singen
chang
drömen
zuo meng
beden
qi dao
snuteln
qin wen

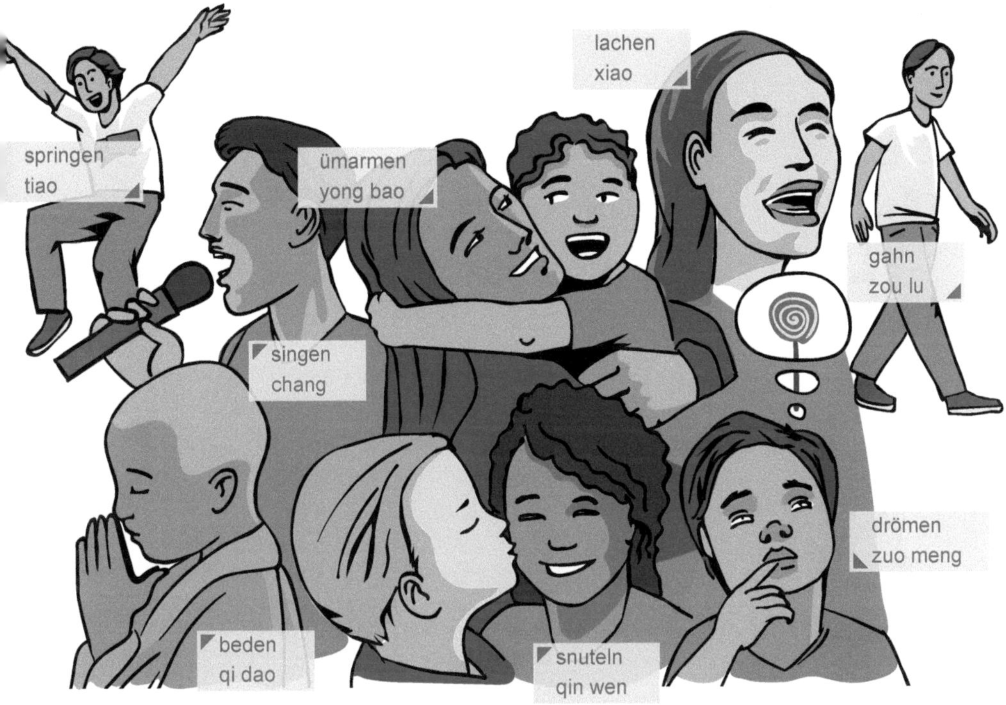

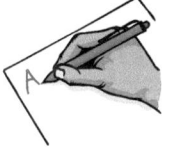

schrieven
shu xie

teken
hua

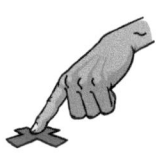

wiesen
zhan shi

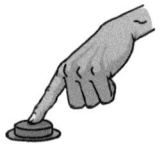

drücken
tui

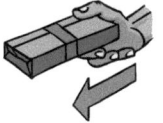

geven
gei

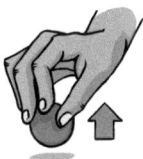

nehmen
na

hebben

you

doon

zuo

sien

dang

stahn

zhan

lopen

pao

trecken

la

smieten

reng

fallen

shuai dao

liggen

tang

töven

deng dai

dregen

xie dai

sitten

zuo

antrecken

chuan yi

slapen

shui jiao

opwaken

xing lai

ankieken

kan

wenen

ku

eien

fu mo

kämmen

shu tou

snacken

jiao tan

verstahn

ming bai

fragen

wen

hören

ting

drinken

he

eten

chi

oprümen

qing li

leefhebben

ai

kaken

zuo fan

fohren

kai che

flegen

fei

segeln

hang xing

reken

ji suan

lesen

du

lehren

xue xi

arbeiden

gong zuo

de Plünnen tohoopsmieten

jie hun

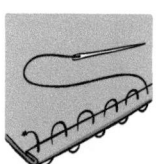

neihen

feng

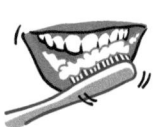

Tähnen putzen

shua ya

dootmaken

sha

smöken

chou yan

schicken

ji

Familje
jia

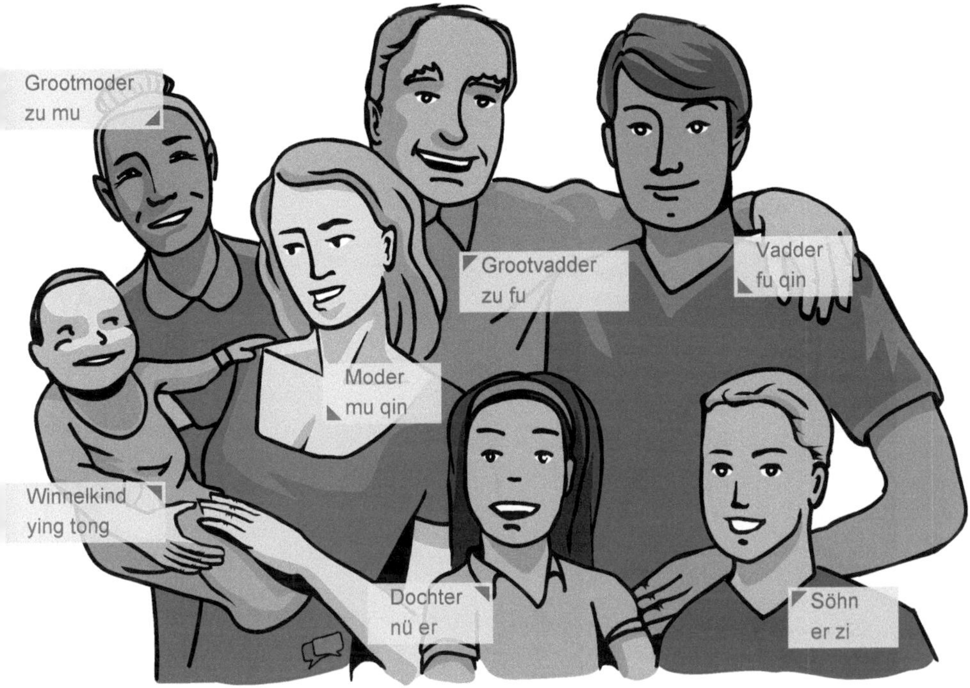

Grootmoder
zu mu
Grootvadder
zu fu
Vadder
fu qin
Moder
mu qin
Winnelkind
ying tong
Dochter
nü er
Söhn
er zi

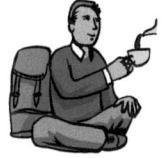

Gast

ke ren

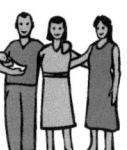

Tant

a yi

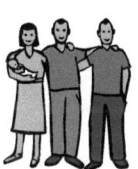

Unkel

shu shu

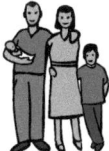

Broder

xiong di

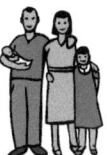

Süster

jie mei

Lief

shen ti

Vörkopp
qian e
Oog
yan jing
Schuller
jian bang
Finger
shou zhi
Gesicht
lian
Kinn
xia ba
Hand
shou
Been
tui
Bost
ru fang
Arm
shou bi

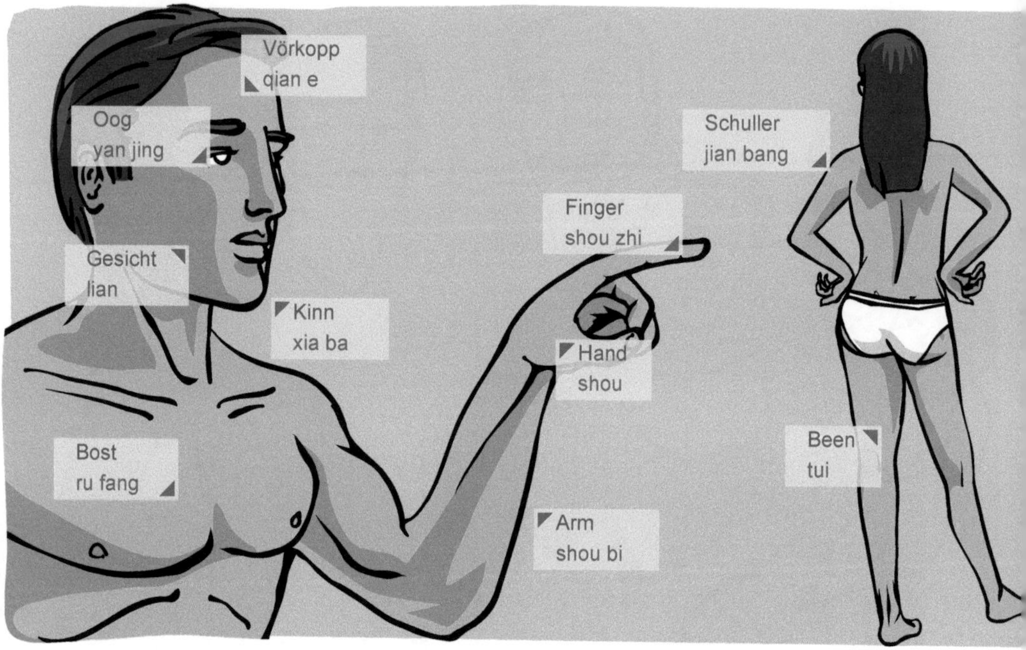

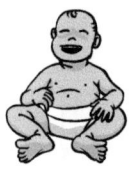

Winnelkind

ying tong

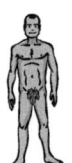

Mann

nan ren

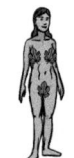

Fro

nü ren

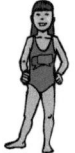

Deern

nü hai

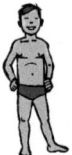

Jung

nan hai

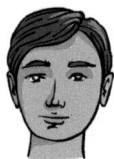

Arm

tou

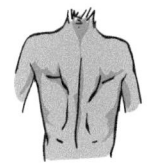

Rüch

bei bu

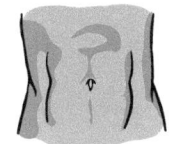

Buuk

du zi

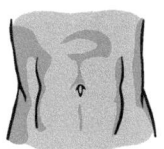

Navel

du qi

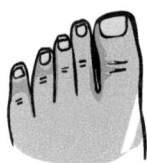

Teh

jiao zhi

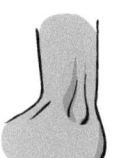

Hack

jiao hou gen

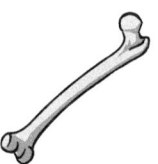

Knaken

gu tou

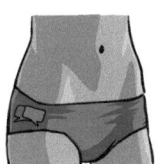

Hüft

tun bu

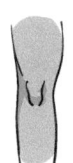

Knee

xi gai

Ellbagen

shou zhou

Nees

bi zi

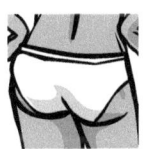

Achtersen

pi gu

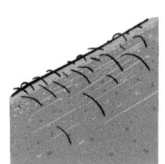

Huut

pi fu

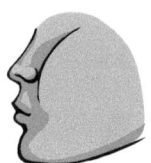

Back

lian jia

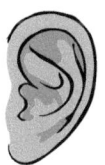

Ohr

er duo

Lipp

zui chun

Mund

zui

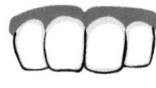

Tähn

ya chi

Tung

she tou

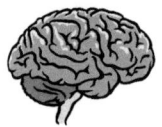

Bregen

nao

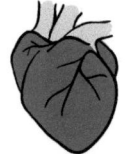

Hart

xin zang

Muskel

ji rou

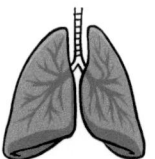

Lung

fei

Lever

gan zang

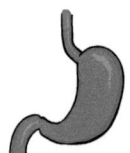

Maag

wei

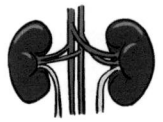

Neren

shen zang

Bislaap

xing jiao

Kondoom

bi yun tao

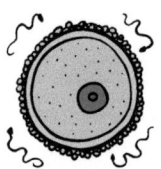

Eizell

luan zi

Sperma

jing zi

Anner Ümstänn

huai yun

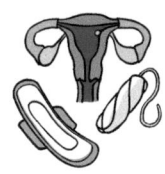

Menstruatschoon
....
yue jing

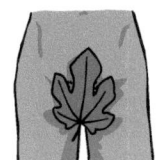

Scheed
....
yin dao

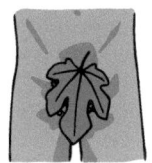

Pint
....
yin jing

Ogenbroe
....
mei mao

Hoor
....
tou fa

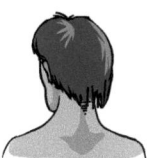

Hals
....
bo zi

Krankenhuus
yi yuan

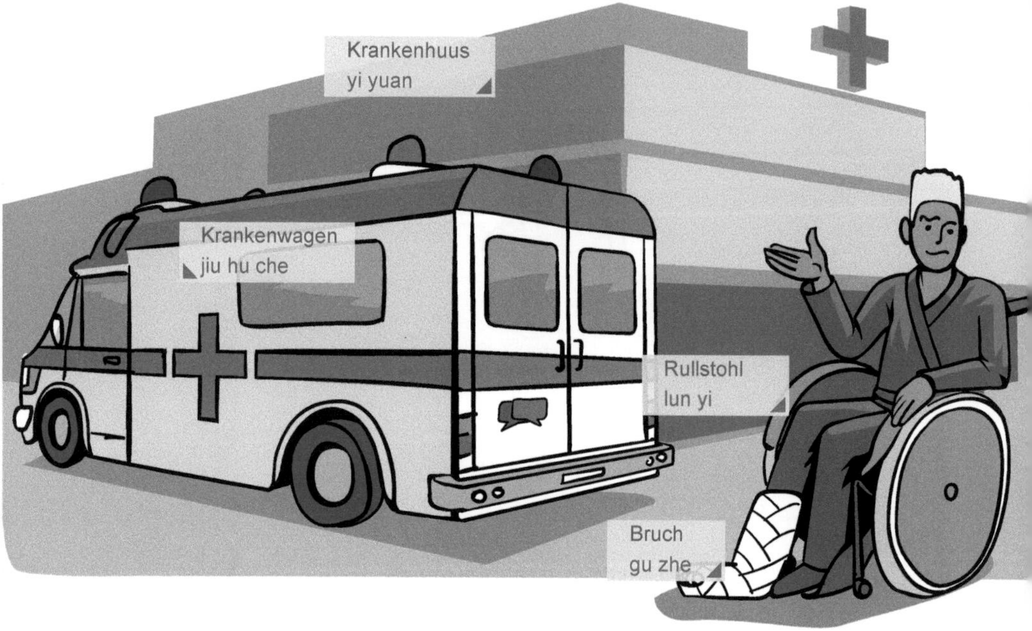

Krankenhuus
yi yuan

Krankenwagen
jiu hu che

Rullstohl
lun yi

Bruch
gu zhe

Dokter

yi sheng

Nootopnahm

ji zhen shi

Krankensüster

hu shi

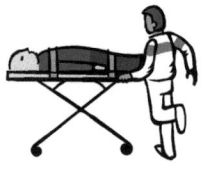

Nootfall

jin ji qing kuang

ahnmächtig

hun mi

Wehdaag

tong

Verwunnen

shou shang

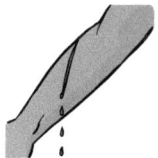

Blöden

chu xue

Hartinfarkt

xin zang bing fa zuo

Slaganfall

zhong feng

Allergie

guo min

Hoosten

ke sou

Fever

fa shao

Gripp

liu gan

Dörchfall

fu xle

Koppwehdaag

tou tong

Kreeft

ai zheng

Zuckersüük

tang niao bing

Chirurg

wai ke yi sheng

Chirurgsch Mess

shou shu dao

Operatschoon

shou shu

CT

CT

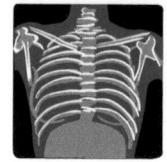

Dörchlüchten

X guang

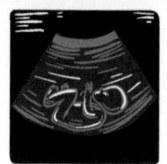

Ultraschall

chao sheng bo

Mask

kou zhao

Krankheit

ji bing

Töövruum

hou zhen shi

Krück

guai zhang

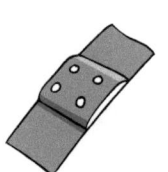

Plaaster

shi gao

Verband

beng dai

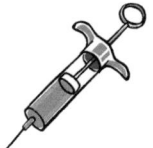

Insprütten

zhu she

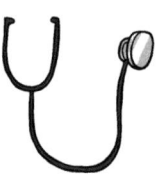

Stethoskop

ting zhen qi

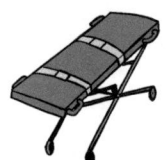

Draag

dan jia

Feverthermometer

ti wen ji

Geboort

chu sheng

Övergewicht

chao zhong

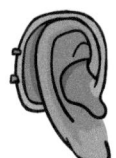

Höörapparat

zhu ting qi

Kiemfriemiddel

xiao du ye

Ansteken

gan ran

Virus

bing du

HIV / AIDS

ai zi bing

Heelmiddel

yao wu

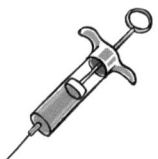

Impen

jie zhong yi miao

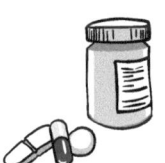

Tabletten

yao pian

Pill

yao wan

Nootroop

ji jiu dian hua

Blootdruck-Meter

xue ya ji

krank / gesund

sheng bing/jian kang

Hölp!

jiu ming!

Alarm

jing bao

Överfall

tu ji

Angreep

gong ji

Gefohr

wei xian

Nootutgang

jin ji chu kou

Füer!

zhao huo la!

Füerlöscher

mie huo qi

Unfall

yi wai

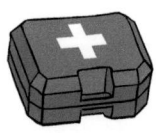

Noothölpkoffer

ji jiu xiang

SOS

hu jiu xin hao

Polizei

jing cha

Europa

ou zhou

Noordamerika

bei mei zhou

Süüdamerika

nan mei zhou

Afrika

fei zhou

Asien

ya zhou

Australien

ao zhou

Atlantik

da xi yang

Pazifik

tai ping yang

Indisch Weltmeer

yin du yang

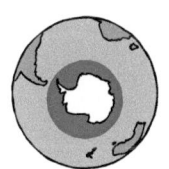

Antarktisch Weltmeer

nan bing yang

Arktisch Weltmeer

bei bing yang

Noordpol

bei ji

Süüdpol
....
nan ji

Antarktis
....
nan ji zhou

Eerd
....
di qiu

Land
....
lu di

See
....
hai

Eiland
....
dao

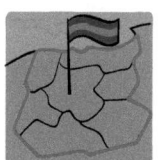

Natschoon
....
guo jia

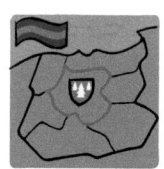

Staat
....
guo jia

Tallenblatt

zhong mian

Stunnenwieser

shi zhen

Minutenwieser

fen zhen

Sekunnenwieser

miao zhen

Wo laat is dat?

xian zai ji dian?

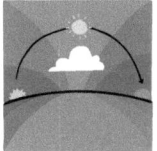

Dag

tian

Tiet

shi jian

nu

xian zai

digetaalsch Klock

dian zi biao

Minuut

fen

Stunn

shi

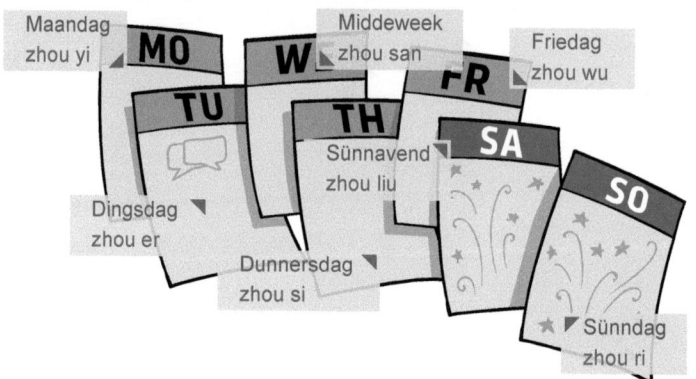

Maandag zhou yi

Middeweek zhou san

Friedag zhou wu

Dingsdag zhou er

Sünnavend zhou liu

Dunnersdag zhou si

Sünndag zhou ri

güstern

zuo tian

hüüt

jin tian

morgen

ming tian

Morgen

zao chen

Meddag

zhong wu

Avend

wan shang

Arbeitsdaag

gong zuo ri

Wekenenn

zhou mo

Johr
nian

Regen
yu
Regenbagen
cai hong
Snee
xue
Wind
feng
Fröhjohr
chun
Harvst
qiu
Sommer
xia
Winter
dong

4.APRIL 11°
5.APRIL 4°
6.APRIL 13°
7.APRIL 8°
8.APRIL 10°

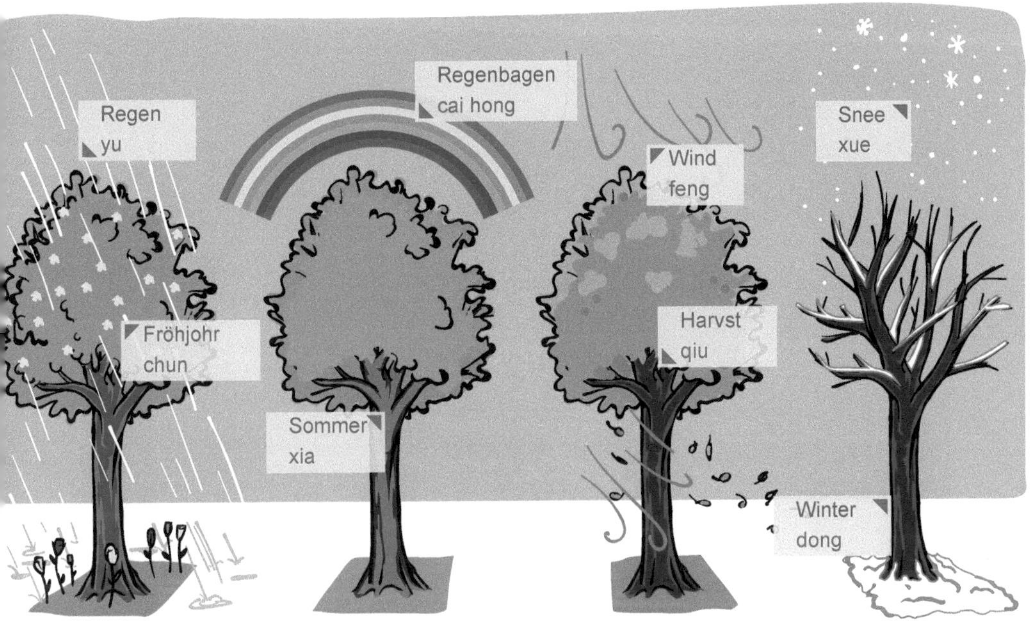

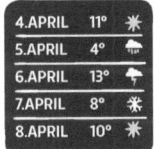

Wedervörhersaag

tian qi yu bao

F C
120 40
90 30
60 20
30 10
0 0
-30 -10
-20

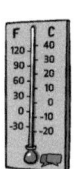

Thermometer

wen du ji

Sünnenschien

yang guang

Wulk

yun

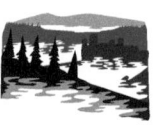

Nevel

wu

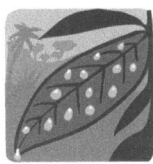

Luftfuchtigkeit

chao shi

Blitz

shan dian

Dunner

da lei

Storm

feng bao

Hagel

bing bao

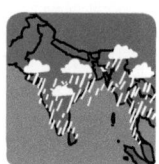

Monsun

ji feng

Floot

hong shui

Ies

bing

Januormaand

yi yue

Februormaand

er yue

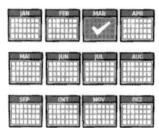

Martmaand

san yue

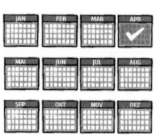

Aprilmaand

si yue

Maimaand

wu yue

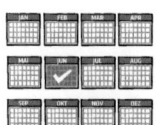

Junimaand

liu yue

Julimaand

qi yue

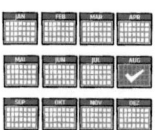

Augustmaand

ba yue

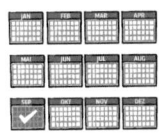

Septembermaand

jiu yue

Oktobermaand

shi yue

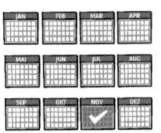

Novembermaand

shi yi yue

Dezembermaand

shi er yue

Formen

xing zhuang

Krink

yuan xing

Quadrat

zheng fang xing

Rechteck

chang fang xing

Dreeeck

san jiao xing

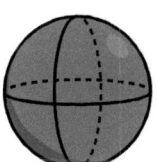

Kugel

qiu ti

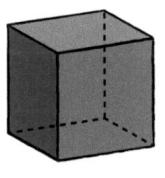

Wörpel

li fang ti

witt

bai

geel

huang

orangsch

cheng

pink

fen

root

hong

lila

zi

blau

lan

gröön

lü

bruun

zong

gries

hui

swart

hei

veel / wenig

hen duo/shao xu

böös / verdreeglich

sheng qi/ping jing

smuck / mies

mei/chou

Begünn / Enn

shou/wei

groot / lütt

da/xiao

hell / düüster

ming/an

Broder / Süster

xiong di/jie mei

schier / schietig

gan jing/ang zang

kumpleet / nich kumpleet

wan zheng/que shi

Dag / Nacht

bai tian/wan shang

doot / lebennig

si/sheng

breet / small

kuan/zhai

geneetbor / nich geneetbor

ke shi yong/fei shi yong

böös / fründlich

xie e/shan liang

fickerig / langwielt

xing fen/wu liao

dick / dünn

pang/shou

toeerst / toletzt

di yi/zui hou

Fründ / Fiend

peng you/di ren

vull / leddig

man/kong

hart / week

ying/ruan

swoor / licht

zhong/qing

Smacht / Döst

e/ke

krank / gesund

sheng bing/jian kang

nich na't Recht / na't Recht

fei fa/he fa

klook / dummerhaftig

cong ming/yu ben

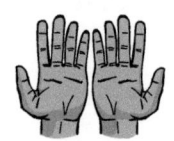

linkerhand / rechterhand

zuo/you

neeg / feern

jin/yuan

nieg / bruukt

xin/jiu

nix / wat

mei you/you xie

oolt / jung

lao/you

an / ut

kai/guan

apen / slaten

da kai/he shang

lies / luut

an jing/chao nao

riek / arm

fu/qiong

richtig / verkehrt

dui/cuo

ruug / glatt

cu cao/guang hua

trurig / glücklich

shang xin/gao xing

kort / lang

duan/chang

suutje / flink

man/kuai

natt / dröög

shi/gan

warm / köhl

wen nuan/liang shuang

Krieg / Freden

zhan zheng/he ping

0

null

ling

1

een

yi

2

twee

er

3

dree

san

4

veer

si

5

fief

wu

6

söss

liu

7

söven

qi

8

acht

ba

9

negen

jiu

10

teihn

shi

11

ölven

shi yi

12	13	14
twölf	dörteihn	veerteihn
shi er	shi san	shi si

15	16	17
föffteihn	sössteihn	söventeihn
shi wu	shi liu	shi qi

18	19	20
achtteihn	negenteihn	twintig
shi ba	shi jiu	er shi

100	1.000	1.000.000
hunnert	dusend	million
bai	qian	bai wan

Engelsch

ying yu

Amerikaansch Engelsch

mei shi ying yu

Chineesch Mandarin

pu tong hua

Hindi

yin di yu

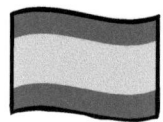

Spaansch

xi ban ya yu

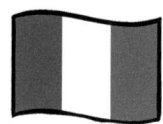

Franzöösch

fa yu

Araabsch

a la bo yu

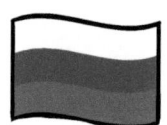

Rusch

e yu

Portugiesch

pu tao ya yu

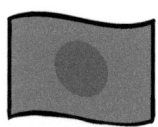

Bengaalsch

feng jia la yu

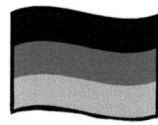

Düütsch

de yu

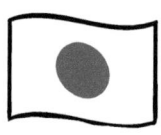

Japaansch

ri yu

ik
....
wo

du
....
ni

he / se / dat
....
ta/ta/ta

wi
....
wo men

ji
....
ni men

se
....
ta men

keen?
....
shei?

wat?
....
shen me?

woans?
....
zen yang?

woneem?
....
na li?

wannehr?
....
shen me shi hou?

Naam
....
ming zi

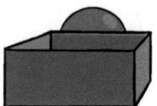

achter

hou mian

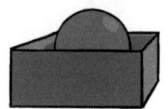

in

li mian

vör

qian mian

över

shang fang

op

shang mian

ünner

xia mian

blangen

pang bian

twüschen

zhong jian

Oort

di dian